LIGHTNING BOLT BOOKS™

W9-AAV-418

It's Rainy Today

Kristin Sterling

Lerner Publications Company
Minneapolis

Dedicated to puddle splashers of all ages

Lerner Publications Company
A division of Lerner Publishing Group, Inc.
241 First Avenue North
Minneapolis, MN 55401 U.S.A.

Website address: www.lernerbooks.com

Library of Congress Cataloging-in-Publication Data

Sterling, Kristin.
    It's Rainy Today / by Kristin Sterling.
        p.   cm. — (Lightning bolt books™—What's the Weather Like?)
    Includes bibliographical references and index.
    ISBN 978-0-7613-4257-1 (lib. bdg. : alk. paper)
    1. Rain and rainfall—Juvenile literature. I. Title.
  QC924.7.S744 2010
    551.577—dc22   2008051586

Manufactured in the United States of America
1 2 3 4 5 6 — BP — 15 14 13 12 11 10

Contents

Drip, Drop, Plop!

Dark, gray clouds form in the sky. Clouds are made of water droplets.

Water droplets cluster in these clouds above a rain forest.

Water droplets combine and become heavy. Soon water falls to the ground as rain.

Rain can fall gently and
quietly in a drizzle.

You can splash barefoot in puddles!

Rain can fall hard and fast in a downpour. You can snuggle up safe indoors.

A rainy day is the perfect time to read a favorite book.

When Does It Rain?

Rain falls in the soggy springtime. The rain helps green plants grow.

Rain helps the plants in this garden thrive.

Flowers blossom. The world fills with growing things.

Rain falls in the frosty winter.
This is called sleet.

Sleet has fallen and frozen on these tree limbs.

Sleet makes the streets
and sidewalks icy!
Take it nice and slow!

Rain falls during thunderstorms. Lightning streaks across the darkened sky.

Rainbows sometimes form after thunderstorms.

BOOM! Thunder roars and the house trembles. Rain washes the earth clean.

Rainy Day Behavior

Sometimes when it rains, earthworms crawl out of their dirt homes.

You can find earthworms on the ground after a rainfall.

Butterflies dangle
underneath leaves.

Orangutans shelter themselves with leaf umbrellas.

An orangutan hides under a leaf during a rainstorm.

Boys and girls put on rubber raincoats and boots.

A Watery World

Some rain falls into the lakes, rivers, and oceans. The sun heats the water, and it becomes vapor.

Vapor rises back into the sky and forms clouds. Rain falls from the clouds again. This is called the water cycle.

Water vapor rises off a river in Colorado.

Sometimes it does not rain for weeks or months. This causes a drought.

Plants wither and die without water.

These grasses have dried out and turned yellow due to a drought.

Sometimes it rains too much.
This causes a flood.

Floods can ruin houses.

Floodwaters can leave homes soggy and badly damaged.

Rain on the Brain

Scientists measure how much rain has fallen. They use a tool called a rain gauge.

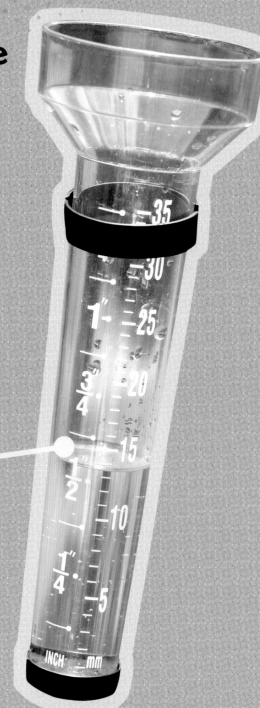

Water has collected in this rain gauge. Checking how much water is inside a rain gauge can tell you how much it has rained.

Boys and girls can also measure rainfall.

Measuring rainfall can help gardeners know if they need to water their plants.

Another Rainy Day

Dark clouds clear away and stars shine in the night sky. Another rainy day has ended.

What will you do on the next rainy day?

27

Activity
You Can Make a Rain Gauge

Do you want to measure how much rain falls in your area? You can make a rain gauge with a few simple items.

What you need:

clear packing tape

a ruler

a clear glass jar

string

a notebook and pencil

What you do:

Create the rain gauge by taping the ruler to the outside of the glass jar. Make sure the ruler is lined up with the bottom of the jar.

Put the jar outside. Use the string to tie the jar to something sturdy so that it does not tip over.

After it rains, check your new rain gauge to see how many inches or centimeters of rain fell. Then use your notebook and pencil to record the date and the amount of rain that fell.

Empty the rain gauge, and place it outside again.

Check the rain gauge each time it rains!

Glossary

droplet: a small drop

drought: a period of dry weather

flood: a flow of water that rises and spreads onto land

rain gauge: a tool for measuring rainfall

sleet: partly frozen rain that falls during cold weather

vapor: water in gas form

Further Reading

Branley, Franklyn M. *Down Comes the Rain.* New York: HarperCollins Publishers, 1997.

D.C. Water and Sewer Authority for Kids
http://www.dcwasa.com/kids

Hesse, Karen. *Come On, Rain!* New York: Scholastic Press, 1999.

Martin, Bill, Jr., and John Archambault. *Listen to the Rain.* New York: H. Holt, 1988.

The Water Cycle
http://www.epa.gov/safewater/kids/flash/flash_watercycle.html

Weather Dude
http://www.wxdude.com

Index

Photo Acknowledgments

The images in this book are used with the permission of: © Jean Louis Batt/Photographer's Choice/Getty Images, pp. 1, 17; © blue jean images/Getty Images, p. 2; © Pegasus/Visuals Unlimited, Inc., p. 4; © Jacques Jangoux/Visuals Unlimited, Inc., p. 5; © Klikk/Dreamstime.com, p. 6; © BananaStock/SuperStock, p. 7; © iStockphoto.com/EricVega, p. 8; © Emilio Ereza/Alamy, p. 9; © Jim Lane/Alamy, p. 10; © Graham Burns/Photofusion Picture Library/Alamy, p. 11; © Jon Van de Grift/Visuals Unlimited, Inc., pp. 12, 20; © Norbert von der Groeben/The Image Works, p. 13; © iStockphoto.com/Pattie Calfy, p. 14; © Ron Niebrugge/Alamy, p. 15; © Anup Shah/naturepl.com, p. 16; © David Epperson/Photodisc/Getty Images, p. 19; © iStockphoto.com/Amanda Rohde, p. 21; © Chris Graythen/Getty Images, p. 22; Dan Callister/Getty Images, p.23; © iStockphoto.com/Mike Clark, p. 24; © age fotostock/SuperStock, p. 25; © Jerry Schad/Photo Researchers, Inc., p. 26; © Woods Wheatcroft/Aurora/Getty Images, p. 27; © Todd Strand/Independent Picture Service, p. 28; © David Frazier/The Image Works, p. 30; © Ariel Skelley/Blend Images/Getty Images, p. 31.

Front cover: © Tom Mareschal/Alamy.